AF300711

OVERCOMING MANIPULATION AT WORK

Put an end to deceit and power games

Written by Adrien de Fraipont
Translated by Rebecca Neal

Coaching 50MINUTES.com

OVERCOMING MANIPULATION AT WORK   9

MANIPULATION AT WORK: THE BASICS   13

What is manipulation?
Manipulation in the context of interpersonal interaction
Recognising manipulation
Getting out of a toxic relationship

TOP TIPS   35

FAQS   39

Who are manipulators?
How can I identify a pathological manipulator at work?
Am I being manipulated at work?
Am I subconsciously contributing to the situation?
When do I need to take action against manipulation?
How can I get out of a manipulative situation?
What laws are there to protect against this kind of abuse?
How can I talk about the situation to the people around me?
How can I help others to overcome manipulation?

OVER TO YOU   49

FURTHER READING   53

OVERCOMING MANIPULATION AT WORK

- **Problem:** how can you defuse situations involving manipulation in the workplace in order to establish a healthier atmosphere without power games between colleagues?
- **Uses:** defending yourself against manipulation at work is a way of working on your assertiveness and improving your relationships with your colleagues and managers.
- **Professional context:** professional relationships with employers, colleagues and subordinates, as manipulation can occur in any sector regardless of the relationship between those involved.
- **FAQs:**
  - Who are manipulators?
  - How can I identify a pathological manipulator at work?
  - Am I being manipulated at work?

- Am I subconsciously contributing to the situation?
- When do I need to take action against manipulation?
- How can I get out of a manipulative situation?
- What laws are there to protect against this kind of abuse?
- How can I talk about the situation to the people around me?
- How can I help others to overcome manipulation?

Any one of us could end up involved in manipulation in the workplace, whether as a witness, the person being manipulated or even the manipulator. Indeed, given how frequent this phenomenon is in interpersonal relationships, you have almost certainly already experienced this kind of situation. For example, you may have felt forced to agree to someone else's request out of fear of disappointing or upsetting them, or you may have used emotional blackmail to get something out of a loved one. Whether consciously or not, we can all end up playing the role of the manipulator or the victim – sometimes during the course of a single conversation.

Power games are an everyday occurrence in our interactions with other people, and especially at work, where people's different positions in the hierarchy add an extra layer of complexity to interpersonal relationships. Although these situations are certainly irritating, as long as they remain reasonably infrequent and minor in nature, they are not necessarily harmful. Real problems only emerge when these attempts to undermine someone else occur repeatedly over an extended period of time.

In this guide, we will provide a more precise definition of manipulation in the workplace, explain the mechanisms behind it, show you how to identify manipulative manoeuvres and offer solutions to thwart any attempts to manipulate you, or to get out of the situation if you are already being manipulated.

MANIPULATION AT WORK: THE BASICS

WHAT IS MANIPULATION?

Manipulation is a behavioural dynamic between two people or groups of people in which one or both sides make a conscious effort to gain the upper hand over the other in order to get their way, generally without the victim realising. The manipulator's conscious aim is therefore to psychologically dominate the other person, and they take great care to ensure that their manoeuvring is not discovered by their potential victims or by a third party. Manipulation is an insidious process of social influence, and is often difficult to detect.

To begin with, it is important to distinguish between manipulation itself and manipulative personalities. A person who is otherwise balanced and reasonable may occasionally try to manipulate someone else for various reasons, whereas a manipulative person is always on the lookout for people to manipulate to achieve their personal goals. Although these "serial manipulators", who feed on the emotions and mental energy of the people around them, are relatively rare, it is important to be able to detect them in order to protect yourself against them. Indeed, manipulation can have serious and even disastrous consequences for victims (loss of job, loss of self-esteem, impact on family life, health problems, and so on) if they do not realise that they are being manipulated in time.

What is specific about manipulation in the workplace?

A range of situations at work provide a breeding ground for manipulation. This is especially true of very competitive industries, where external pressure risks encouraging this kind of behaviour.

Different situations of manipulation are possible in the workplace:

- **A manager or supervisor manipulates their subordinate.** A boss may try to manipulate one of their employees into doing things that breach the terms or the spirit of their contract.

- **A subordinate manipulates their manager.** Conversely, an employee may manipulate their superior through flattery, small acts of sabotage or the withholding of information, for example.
- **An employee manipulates one of their colleagues.** One employee may try to manipulate another in order to land a promotion or keep their job at the expense of the other person, for example by subtly undermining their work.
- **An employee manipulates several of their colleagues.** One employee may try to stand out from the group and seem more capable than the others. For example, they may use their charisma to become the informal leader of the group and use the others for their own ends.

ADVICE FOR EMPLOYERS

Manipulation at work can result in tensions between colleagues and hamper the company's internal efficiency. If a manipulative person sabotages the work of their victim(s), possibly through wrongdoing that the other person is then blamed for, or if a person's self-confidence and motivation are undermined to such a point that they are no longer able to do their work, it is in the employer's best interests to take action.

MANIPULATION IN THE CONTEXT OF INTERPERSONAL INTERACTION

The Karpman drama triangle

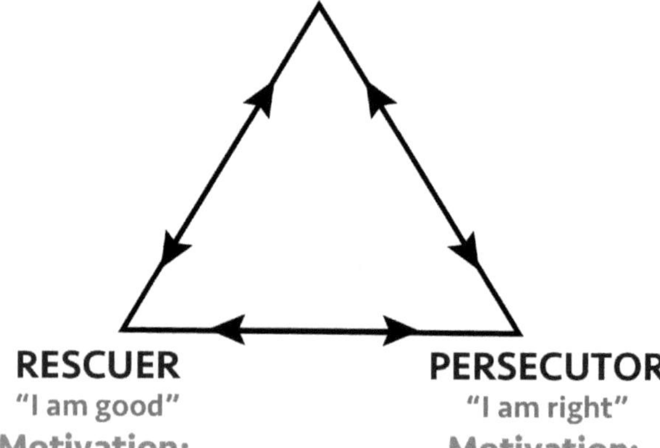

The Karpman drama triangle, which outlines the roles of Victim, Rescuer and Persecutor and illustrates the interplay between them, is instructive when we are looking to understand the phenomenon of manipulation. According to this theory, developed by the psychologist Stephen Karpman, we tend to adopt particular roles in our relationships based on our personal motivations and the roles that other people play. We generally have a preferred role, but we may take on another depending on the situation.

Karpman identifies three very different roles:

- The **Persecutor**, whose main goal is to overwhelm and dominate others in order to protect themselves early on in the relationship, and who does not hesitate to trample others under foot. They build themselves up at the expense of other people.
- The **Victim**, who is looking for security and protection and who yields their share of the responsibility to the other person. They constantly feel that they are putting up with things and being attacked, and think that there is nothing they can to do to change the situation. From the outside, this may seem

like a comfortable position, but it conceals profound self-abnegation.
- The **Rescuer**, who likes to shout their acceptance and love for other people from the rooftops. They are quick to rush to the assistance of others, which can be infantilising.

Taking on one of these roles, whether consciously or subconsciously, allows us to impose ourselves on other people without giving them the chance to say no. This not only negatively impacts how we view ourselves, but also forces the other person to play a particular role. In reality, each of the three roles is a form of manipulation which aims to allow us to get what we want:

- The Persecutor openly imposes themselves and pushes the other person into the Victim role, so that they will agree to their requests without putting up a fight.
- The Victim's self-pity encourages the other person to take on the Rescuer role and give in to their requests so as not to feel bad about themselves. However, in the long run a person playing the Victim risks awakening the Persecutor who lies dormant in all of us.
- The Rescuer has no qualms about meddling

in other people's lives and pushing them into the Victim role so that they need help and are indebted to the person who has saved them.

RECOGNISING MANIPULATION

Whether we are dealing with an inveterate or an occasional manipulator, at first glance they tend to seem pleasant and likeable. They flatter their victim and try to befriend them, for example by inviting them for a drink after work. They use this opportunity to get to know their target better, to put up a selfless façade and to offer to lend a hand with a range of tasks (in short, they present themselves as a Rescuer), but in reality that are trying to manoeuvre their way into a position of authority by subtly drawing attention to their own knowledge and skills. Their goal is entirely selfish: they are trying to gradually encroach on their victim's "mental real estate".

Once contact has been established, the manipulator has several weapons in their arsenal to exert a hold over their victim: deliberately vague communication, making the victim feel inferior or guilty, and even establishing a climate of fear, which will have emotional effects that are difficult for the other person to manage.

Vague communication

Manipulators use verbal and nonverbal language to capture their victim's attention and deprive them of their freedom (Petitcollin 2008). If you pay close attention, their way of talking, their attitudes and their gestures betray their intention to manipulate.

With regard to verbal communication:

- The manipulator communicates in a disordered way, so it is impossible to pin down their needs, requests, opinions, and so on. Similarly, they generally give vague responses to questions related to their personality or to subjects that they are not an expert on, in order to give the impression that they know the answers but do not want to talk about the topic at length. This allows them to remain on their pedestal above other people.
- They use the volume of their voice to monopolise other people's attention, either by speaking so loudly that nobody can speak over them, or by speaking so quietly that everyone

else has to stop talking in order to hear them.

- The manipulator tells lies in order to get at the truth. For example, they may ask a question with deliberately false information in order to learn more about their victim.
- They steal other people's ideas and either claim that they had them first or feign ignorance.
- They have no qualms about lying to get what they want, for example by claiming that they never asked a particular question. Their vague communication makes this easier for them.
- They regularly communicate through intermediaries in order to give themselves more room for manoeuvre. This makes it easier to go back on what they have said by claiming that there has been a misunderstanding due to the messenger.

THE DOUBLE BIND

Manipulators often use a technique known as the double bind. This refers to a suggestion which contains a paradoxical double message, so that if one message is obeyed the other is necessarily disobeyed, and vice versa. The typical example is asking someone to volunteer to do something: if they have had to be asked, it is not voluntary!

With regard to nonverbal communication:

- The manipulator displays a striking lack of empathy, which is linked to their condescending attitude towards their target and has specific nonverbal manifestations. For example, they either do not make eye contact or try to stare down the other person, and when somebody talks to them they do not turn towards them, but simply carry on with what they are doing while they listen without even looking at the other person.
- The manipulator is "out of sync" with other people. For example, in a meeting where everyone else is listening carefully and taking notes, they sit back in their chair and do not write anything down as a way of positioning themselves above other people.
- When they are criticised, they smile so as to always seem sure of themselves.

Fuelling feelings of inferiority

Having placed themselves in a position of authority over their victim, the manipulator works to make them doubt themselves and lose their old confidence in themselves and their abilities. To do this, the manipulator feigns surprise at some of their victim's comments (for example if they say that their manager has praised their work), minimises their words or actions, gives them condescending nicknames, gives veiled criticism and acts in bad faith. As a result, the victim feels that they have lost their credibility, starts doubting their own abilities and thinks that they will never be good enough.

One of the manipulator's most frequently used techniques is implying that the other person is lying, when really they are the one deceiving their victim. At the same time, they try to cover their tracks by bombarding the victim with information, whether it is true or not, which leaves them confused. This allows them to present themselves as a Rescuer and the only one who can put things right, which gradually erodes the victim's self-esteem and reinforces their dependence on the manipulator. The manipulator may even encourage their victim to come talk to them, as this allows them to feign sympathy while drawing attention to the other person's weakness.

Playing the victim and blaming the other person

Another common manipulation technique is pretending to be an innocent victim, for example by talking about health problems, an excessive workload, personal issues, and so on. In this case, the manipulator asks for things at the last minute because they "forgot" or because they "don't have time" to deal with them. The "poor manipulator" always gives the appearance of being busy or physically incapable of carrying out certain tasks.

Playing the victim allows people to offload their responsibilities on someone else. Indeed, the manipulator's victim will probably agree to their requests, in this way assuming the Rescuer role, which will subsequently make them more likely to do what the manipulator wants out of a sense of charity. If they refuse, they will feel guilty and as though they are betraying their principles.

Manipulators can also make their target feel guilty about something that they have or have not done and make them feel as though they are the bad one. The manipulator then exploits the feeling of guilt they have created in order to constantly ask for more from their victim, who is more likely to agree to these requests so that they can be forgiven.

At the same time, the manipulator cultivates a respectable image and forges a reputation as an honest, decent person so that nobody suspects their sinister intentions and the victim becomes convinced that they are really the bad guy.

Inspiring fear

The manipulator can also generate a climate of fear to help them get what they want. To go back to Karpman's roles, in this case they are positioning themselves as the Persecutor. They behave in an authoritarian manner and bark orders, claiming that it is urgent. If they are above you in the hierarchy, they abuse their position to constantly ask for more from you by dangling a promotion in front of you or, on the contrary, threatening to take you out of consideration or even to fire you. Blackmail and implicit threats are two more tools that they use to chip away at your willpower.

> **EXAMPLE**
>
> You stay late at work at the expense of your personal life because your colleagues claim to have heard rumours that you are at risk of losing your job.

Furthermore, if you try to stand up to them, they become irritable or even aggressive. They may get angry, and their victim knows this. They can also behave melodramatically, calling to mind the "godfather" figure who makes an offer that you cannot refuse.

GETTING OUT OF A TOXIC RELATIONSHIP

The consequences for the victim

Victims of manipulation are subjected to increasing stress, and can end up physically and emotionally exhausted. In the worst-case scenario, they will suffer psychological damage that it can be difficult to recover from.

Manipulation causes particular problems when it extends beyond the world of work and encroaches on the victim's emotions and family life, or when it has consequences on their health (digestive or breathing difficulties, trouble sleeping, and so on).

In this case, it is essential to identify the origin of the phenomenon and implement a strategy to get out of the situation and protect yourself.

Prevention

The first tip to prevent manipulation is to learn to recognise it for what it is. This will stop you from being truly manipulated, as opposed to being subjected to minor, inconsequential attempts to influence you.

The next step is to continually work on strengthening your interpersonal skills, in order to forge healthy, mature relationships and to avoid falling into the trap of playing a role. This involves self-respect, respect for others, active listening and assertiveness.

INTERPERSONAL SKILLS

- Active listening is a key tool in improving your relationships with other people. This means making yourself available to the person you are talking to, paying attention to them and taking an interest in what they are saying. It is important to understand them and their needs. To do this, you need to try and decode their emotional language, meaning the things that they do not say but still express one way or another. Reformulation and questions are also active listening tools which help or oblige the other person to express their thoughts more precisely.
- Another key element in interpersonal relationships is assertiveness, meaning the ability to clearly express and defend your opinions and needs without infringing the other person's rights. As such, making an assertive request means setting out objective facts, your feelings about these facts and your needs. The request itself

comes afterwards, is presented simply and clearly, and seeks, if not the other person's complete agreement, at least a compromise that satisfies both parties.

Changing the relationship

It is not always easy to escape a manipulator when you are in the thick of the situation. Indeed, the manipulator's hold over their victim means that they may even start to miss them when they break away from them. In this section, we will explain how to get over this feeling.

STOCKHOLM SYNDROME

Stockholm syndrome takes its name from a bank robbery that took place in the Swedish capital in 1973, in which four bank employees were taken hostage. When the hostages were released, they took up their captor's cause and even refused to testify against him in court.

Sympathy for the tormentor is a frequent psychological phenomenon that also occurs in relationships between manipulators and their victims. This adds to the potential difficulty of breaking free of your dependence on your manipulator if you are not adequately prepared.

The first step is to realise that you are being manipulated, now that you have learnt to recognise it. If your relationship with one of your colleagues or your manager is making you uncomfortable, establish some emotional distance from them to give yourself the time to think and review the situation. Can you identify some of the signs of manipulation? Has the situation been going on for some time? If your suspicions turn out to be justified, you can take action to change things.

The second step is to talk about your situation with people you trust. This will give you reassurance and help you find the strength to assert yourself and try to change the situation. That said, do not blow the situation out of proportion or let yourself wallow in self-pity, as this may undermine your credibility.

The third step is to take charge of the situation. If your manipulator is taking advantage of your emotions and your reactions to certain strategies, you also bear some responsibility. Stop letting their scheming affect you and refuse to play the part they want you to play. To do this, set limits and learn to say no if a request crosses them. For example, if the manipulator makes urgent requests to throw you off balance and, potentially, to cause you to make mistakes that they can use against you later on, stop agreeing to do things at the last minute. You also have your schedule at work, and you should stick to it. Tell the manipulator that it was their responsibility to take care of the task in good time and refuse to come to their aid.

Take decisive action against their vague communication: ask them to clarify any imprecise points and, above all, do not lose heart if they rebuff you and suggest that the problem lies with you, not them. In this situation, you could also calmly explain that they have hurt you and that you will not tolerate being belittled in this way.

These steps will allow you to gradually modify your relationship with this person and potentially move towards a healthy relationship free from power games.

Escaping the relationship

On the other hand, if you are dealing with a genuine pathological manipulator (remember, though, that they are rare), there is no way you can establish mature communication with them. In this case, you should simply refuse to engage with them. To do this, practice counter-manipulation. The aim of this approach is to escape their hold over you and show them gradually and subtly that you see through their games and can cope just fine without them.

The first step in counter-manipulation is to stop justifying yourself. Feign indifference, be impersonal and use clichés and bland statements when you talk to them. For example, if they criticise your work, you can respond "You know what they say, practice makes perfect". You can also turn their statements against them ("You said that, not me"), make a joke or use self-deprecation to get out of awkward situations, while remaining calm and courteous.

If you adopt this approach, the manipulator should soon lose interest. If they persist and you cannot ignore them (for example if they are your manager), or if they turn their attentions to a new victim, you will need to report them to HR. In this case, prepare thoroughly, for example by making a note of any agreements you have reached with them or of the impossible deadlines they set for you. Alternatively, you may need to sever ties with them completely, even if this means changing jobs: your mental health is far more important than your work.

TOP TIPS

- **Take the time to understand how manipulation works.** This will give you the basic tools you need to either avoid falling into this trap or to get out of it.
- If you suspect that someone wants to manipulate you, **avoid revealing too much of your personality or too many details about your private life** to them. Skirt around these topics, as the manipulator may use them against you.
- **Follow your intuition.** The manipulator either already has or plans on sowing doubt in your mind. Trust yourself and your instincts!
- **Learn to say no.** You can maintain your self-confidence by learning to refuse requests that you do not want to carry out. Several types of refusal are possible:
  - Partial refusal, which involves only accepting part of the request.
  - Constructive criticism, which you can use if the request is not wholly justified and you want to negotiate terms.
  - Total refusal, when agreeing to any part

of the request is out of the question. If the other person insists, use the "broken record" technique: simply repeat your refusal until they let the matter drop.

- As a general rule, **say no to vague requests or ask the other person to clarify** until everything is clear to you, **refuse to be an intermediary** for other people's requests, **be wary of flattery**, and **pretend to be indifferent** to comments that are clearly intended to hurt you.
- If you have not managed to establish healthy communication with the manipulator, **stop trying to get them to understand you**. They have made it clear that they do not care about your feelings, so there is no point wasting your time trying to talk to them.
- **When the manipulator's behaviour is not even subtle, ridicule it so as to undermine their credibility.** This may throw them off balance and put an end to their scheming.
- **Avoid isolating yourself and talk to the people around you.** Criticise the manipulation you have experienced or that you have witnessed between colleagues. You can also confide in your family and close friends. It is

important for everyone who is being manipulated to have a friendly ear to listen to and understand them, and to have access to the empathy and kindness that the manipulator is denying them.

- **Do not be paranoid!** Just because someone displays a particular manipulative characteristic at one time or another does not mean that they are a serial manipulator. If you are unsure about your relationship with somebody, it is essential to take the time to analyse the situation. The aim of these tips is to help you to establish healthy working relationships that are as free from power games as possible, not to create a climate of generalised mistrust.

FAQS

WHO ARE MANIPULATORS?

Any of us can become a manipulator, through the roles we play and the relationships we have with other people. However, some people have an inherently toxic manipulative personality and are always on the lookout for a new victim. Manipulation is a permanent feature of the way they interact with the people around them.

HOW CAN I IDENTIFY A PATHOLOGICAL MANIPULATOR AT WORK?

If a person displays several of the following characteristics, there is a good chance that they have a manipulative personality, and you should watch out for them:

- a colleague takes up too much or not enough space at work;
- their attitudes and opinions vary depending on the person they are talking to;

- they take a lot of interest in you, but in a condescending way;
- they often pass on messages through intermediaries;
- they are never very clear and act like you are an idiot if you say that you do not understand;
- when you tell them about your feelings, they disregard them;
- they make commitments that they do not stick to;
- they regularly get you to do their work by claiming that it is urgent, that they are overwhelmed, that they have something more important to do or that they are struggling with health problems;
- they constantly complain so that you are tempted to take pity on them;
- nothing you do is ever good enough for them, but they do not help you to improve and keep asking you to carry out the same tasks;
- they blame you for things and nitpick your personality, not your work;
- they are incapable of accepting criticism;
- they lie and badmouth other people;
- their behaviour often does not match up with what they say;

- they use their attitudes and words to give themselves an air of superiority, but they are quick to change the subject or slip away if their ignorance on certain points risks coming to light;
- they seem effective in their work, but you wonder if this is at the expense of other people, or even of your own work.

AM I BEING MANIPULATED AT WORK?

You can work out if you are being manipulated by analysing your discomfort and identifying the repeated manipulative behaviours of one of your colleagues:

- If you are less sure of yourself than when you first started working at your current job, ask yourself why.
- Carry out some self-reflection in order to determine whether you are subject to stress or other physical and mental health issues at work.
- Analyse your workload compared with those of your colleagues and ask yourself whether you are being treated differently.

- If you have suspicions about one of your collea-gues, look more closely at your relationship with them. For example, ask yourself why they seem to have taken a particular liking to you, but often ask you for help with their work.

AM I SUBCONSCIOUSLY CONTRIBUTING TO THE SITUATION?

Undoubtedly. Remember that manipulation takes place in a relationship between two or more people. If you are being manipulated, this means that something in your behaviour is allowing the other person to take advantage of you. For example, have you played the role of a Victim or a Rescuer?

This realisation does not mean that you should blame yourself or put yourself down. In fact, it is a good thing: it means that you have made a mistake, but that you have the power to change the relationship. What are you waiting for?

WHEN DO I NEED TO TAKE ACTION AGAINST MANIPULATION?

The earlier you do something, the easier it will be to stop the manipulator from gaining a hold over you or to escape their clutches. However, it is never too late. Keep in mind that, without their deception and power games, the manipulator's modus operandi will not get them anywhere. Once the first cracks have appeared in their façade, it is easier to adopt an approach which combines counter-attack and defence mechanisms by standing up for yourself and setting limits. In short, as soon as you feel uncomfortable about a particular relationship, it is time to take action.

HOW CAN I GET OUT OF A MANIPULATIVE SITUATION?

- The first step is to identify what kind of manipulative process you are experiencing.
- Establish some emotional distance in order to calmly analyse the potentially toxic relationship.
- Talk about it with people you trust.

- Take action to change the relationship:
  - work on your self-confidence;
  - act like a responsible adult;
  - refuse to play a role;
  - stand up for yourself and state your needs;
  - practice active listening;
  - make assertive requests.
- As a last resort, refuse to engage with the manipulator and use counter-manipulation to protect yourself.

WHAT LAWS ARE THERE TO PROTECT AGAINST THIS KIND OF ABUSE?

In legal terms, repeated, continuous manipulation of an employee, whether or not the manipulator really intends to harm them, falls under the umbrella of bullying and harassment.

If the manipulator's behaviour can be classed as abusive and repeated, and has harmful consequences for you, you are within your rights to take action. The steps to follow are set out below:

- If you cannot reach an agreement informally,

the next step is to make a formal complaint following your employer's procedures. These should tell you who to complain to and how your complaint will be dealt with.

ADVICE FOR EMPLOYERS

Employers are legally responsible for preventing bullying and harassment at work. It may be a good idea to implement a policy on bullying and harassment including, for example, a list of unacceptable behaviours and training for managers.

- After considering your case, your employer may take action to resolve the situation. This could include mediation, counselling or disciplinary action against the bully or harasser.
- If these steps fail, you should seek advice on your legal rights, which will vary depending on your situation.

Acas has produced a guide on bullying and harassment in the workplace featuring definitions, an explanation of employers' responsibilities and your options if you are being bullied or harassed: http://www.acas.org.uk/media/pdf/r/l/Bullying-and-harassment-at-work-a-guide-for-employees.pdf.

HOW CAN I TALK ABOUT THE SITUATION TO THE PEOPLE AROUND ME?

In this kind of situation, you absolutely need support. If you have the opportunity to talk to the people around you about it, explain the facts as objectively as possible and tell them how you feel about the situation. Look for friendly listeners, who will probably not be able to suggest a solution, but will help you to get a better grasp of the situation and think about ways of changing it simply by listening to you. Talk about all the things the manipulator does not want other people to know.

HOW CAN I HELP OTHERS TO OVERCOME MANIPULATION?

The best way of helping other people to overcome manipulation is to listen to them. If you work with the person who is being manipulated, you can also:

- show that you disapprove of the manipulator's actions;
- refer the case to a manager;
- find a qualified person that your colleague can talk to in complete confidence;
- suggest that your colleague seek psychological support.

The essential thing here is that your colleague can consider you an ally and that they feel understood. This will enable them to rebuild their self-confidence.

OVER TO YOU

Think about your personal experience and identify a time when you felt as though you were being manipulated and gave in to another person's desires against your own wishes.

What type of manipulation was it?

- Did you let a Victim move you?
- Did you feel indebted to a Rescuer?
- Were you tormented by a Persecutor?

Why did you let yourself be manipulated?

- Was it to avoid an unpleasant emotion? Is so, what was the emotion?
- Were you afraid of losing something that matters to you (such as your job, for example)? If so, what?
- Conversely, were you hoping to get something out of the situation? If so, what?

What irrational beliefs made you let yourself be manipulated?

- "I have to be perfect."
- "My words and actions have to be consistent."
- "I have to know everything."
- "I can never make mistakes."
- "Everyone has to like me."
- "I have to help other people."
- "I have to have an opinion on everything and never change it."
- "My opinion must be less valid than the other person's".
- Etc.

Answering these questions honestly will teach you about yourself and allow you to understand what motivates you in your relationships with other people. You will then be able to develop your interpersonal skills, which in turn will stop you from getting entangled in toxic relationships, in both your professional and personal life.

We want to hear from you!
Leave a comment on your online library
and share your favourite books on social media!

FURTHER READING

BIBLIOGRAPHY

- Acas. (No date) *Bullying and harassment at work: A guide for employees.* [Online]. [Accessed 17 October 2017]. Available from: <http://www.acas.org.uk/media/pdf/r/l/Bullying-and-harassment-at-work-a-guide-for-employees.pdf>

- Acas. (No date) *Bullying and harassment at work: A guide for managers and employers.* [Online]. [Accessed 17 October 2017]. Available from: <http://www.acas.org.uk/media/pdf/2/j/Bullying-and-harassment-in-the-workplace-a-guide-for-managers-and-employers.pdf>

- Andersen, M. (2014) *La manipulation ordinaire. Reconnaître les relations toxiques pour s'en protéger.* Paris: Marabout.

- Hirigoyen, M-F. (1998) *Le harcèlement moral, la violence perverse au quotidien.* Paris: La Découverte & Syros.

- Milgram, S. (2010) *Obedience to Authority.* New York: HarperCollins.

- Nazare-Aga, I. (2004) *Les manipulateurs sont parmi nous.* Montreal: Les Éditions de l'Homme.

- Petitcollin, C. (2008) *Échapper aux manipulateurs.*

Paris: Guy Trédaniel éditeur.

- Références. (2013) *Harcèlement au travail: notre dossier.* [Online]. [Accessed 17 October 2017]. Available from: <https://references.lesoir.be/en-gb/article/harc%C3%A8lement-au-travail-notre-dossier/?s=7>

ADDITIONAL SOURCES

- Bronckart, V. (2017) *Developing Your Assertiveness.* Trans. Neal, R. Brussels: Plurilingua Publishing.

- Fléron, B. (2017) *Combatting Bullying at Work.* Trans. Neal, R. Brussels: Plurilingua Publishing.

50MINUTES.com
History
Business
Coaching
Book Review
Health & Wellbeing
IMPROVE YOUR
GENERAL KNOWLEDGE
IN A BLINK OF AN EYE !
www.50minutes.com

www.50minutes.com

Ebook EAN: 9782808000451

Paperback EAN: 9782808000468

Legal Deposit: D/2017/12603/450

Cover: © Primento

Digital conception by Primento, the digital partner of publishers.